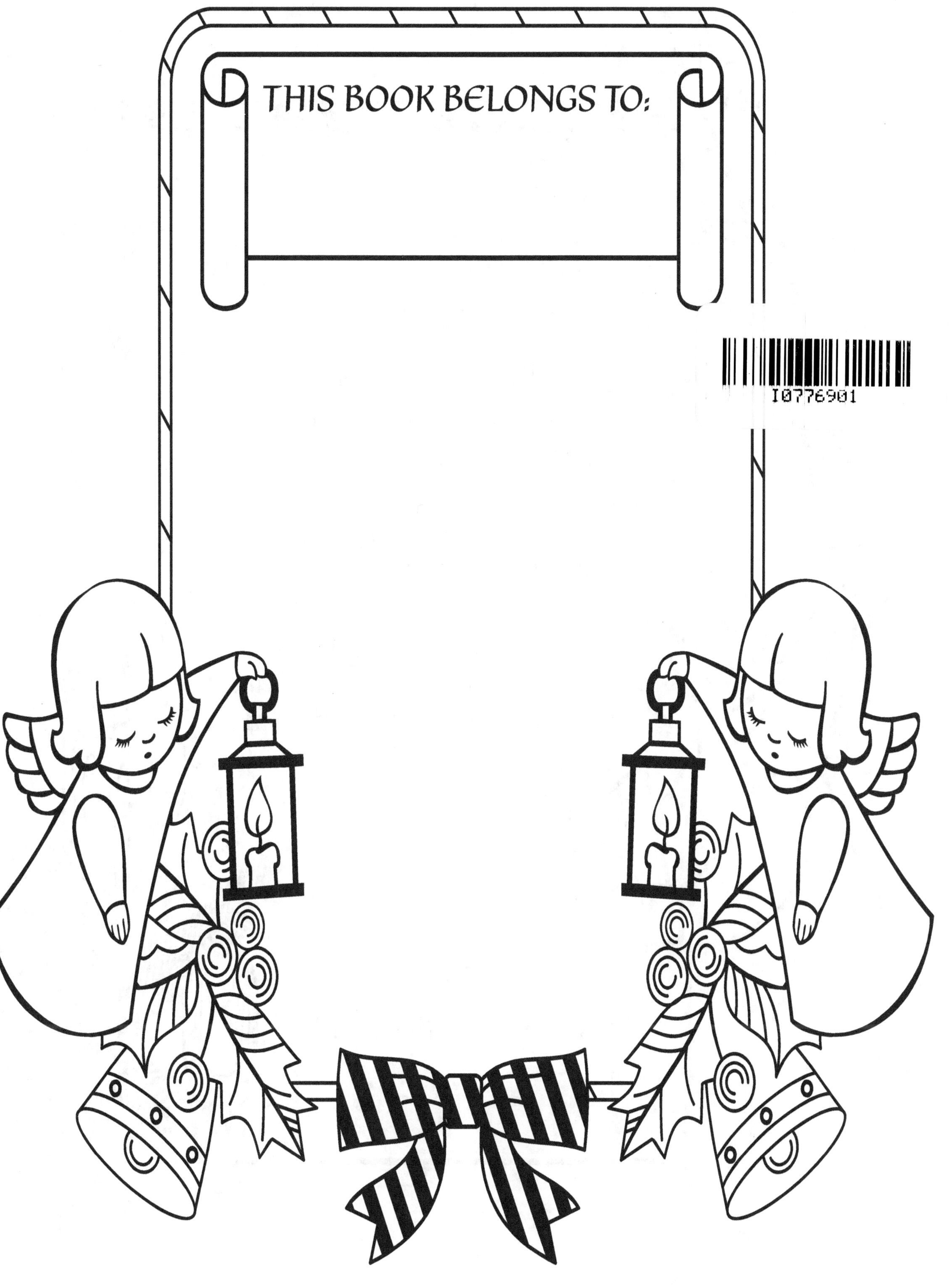
THIS BOOK BELONGS TO:
I0776901

1. There's one activity for every day of Advent.

2. Read the directions carefully before you start each activity.

3. You'll need some supplies: scissors, glue, pencil, crayons, colored pencils, or markers, and extra paper.

4. Some pages take longer, so you may do the pages in any order.

5. Use the Advent calendar on page 56 to color each day of Advent. Then cut out the days and glue them in the correct order on another sheet of paper.

TIPS
FOR USING THIS BOOK!

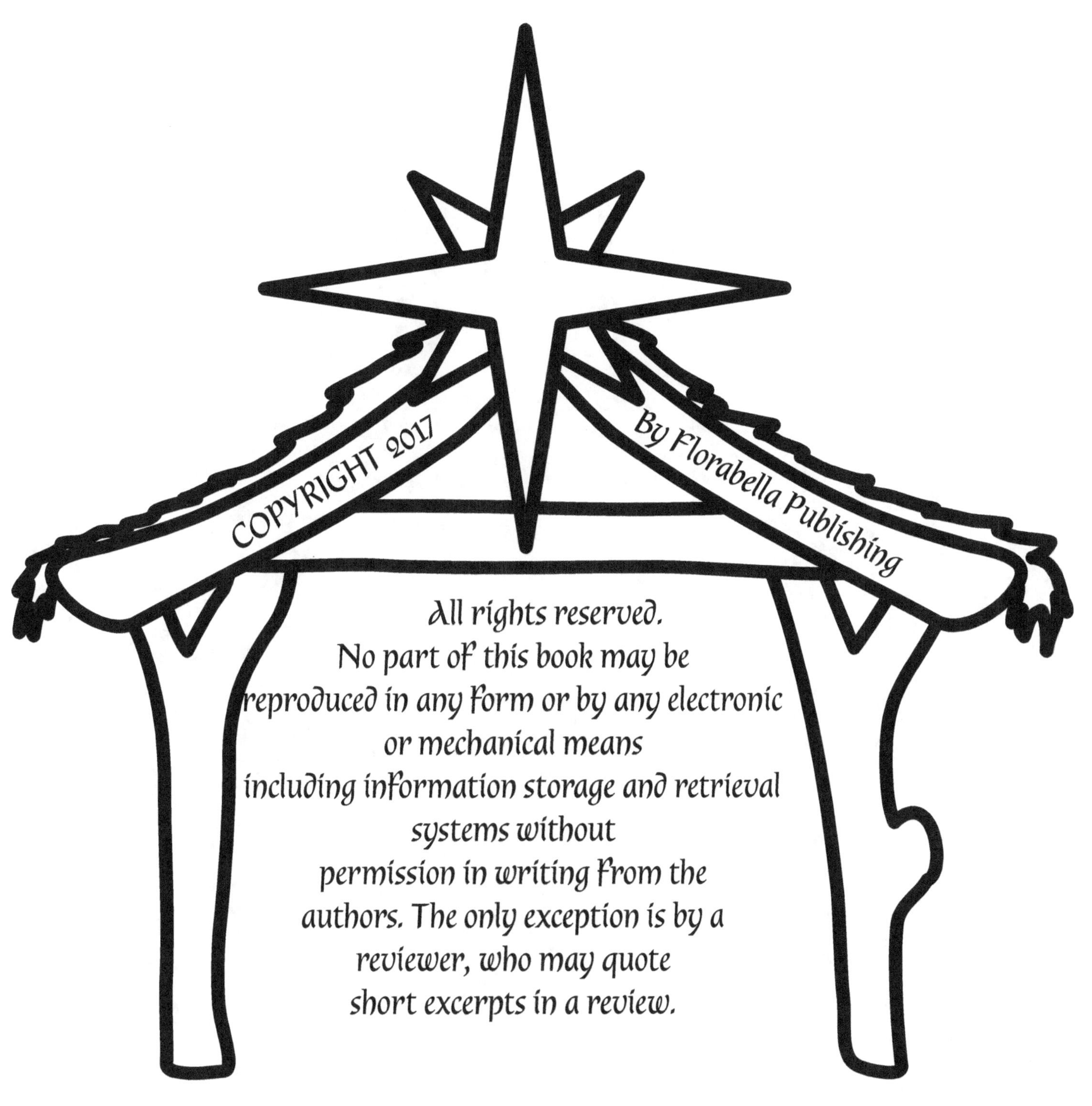

IT'S THE MOST WONDERFUL TIME OF THE YEAR!

DAY 1
Color, cut, and glue the pictures on another sheet of paper to create a Christmas nativity scene.

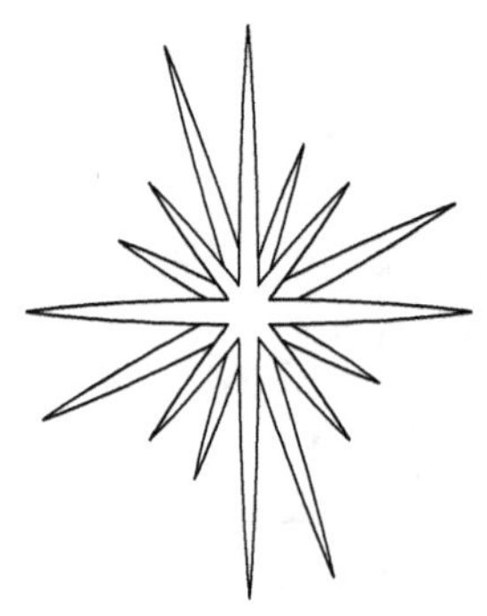

DAY 2 - Color the king!

DAY 3-Complete the reindeer maze.
Hint: Start at the antlers.

DAY 4 - Color, cut, & glue the tree on another sheet of paper.

DAY 5 -Color in the circles as you find the words.

Christmas Word Search

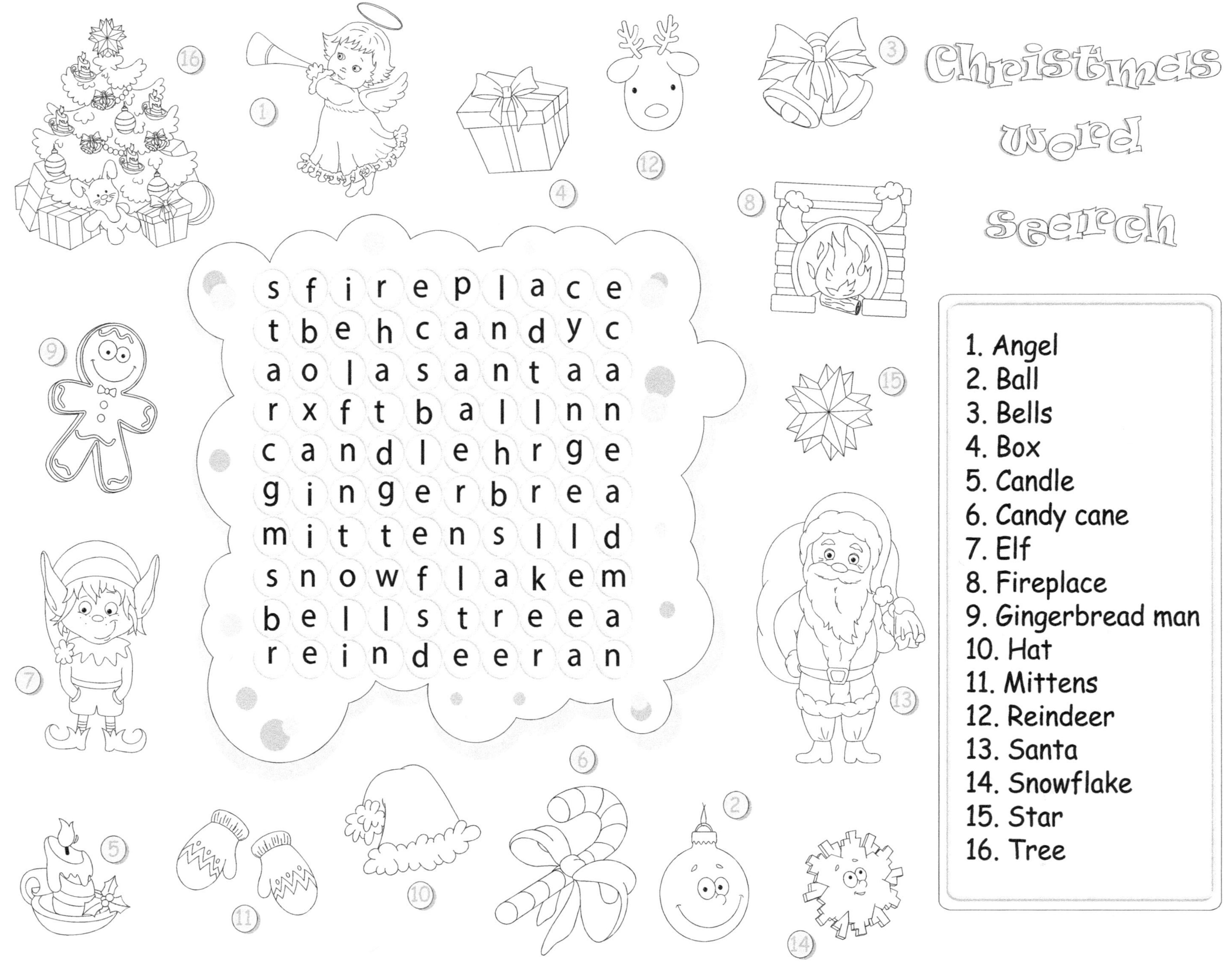

s f i r e p l a c e
t b e h c a n d y c
a o l a s a n t a a
r x f t b a l l n n
c a n d l e h r g e
g i n g e r b r e a
m i t t e n s l l d
s n o w f l a k e m
b e l l s t r e e a
r e i n d e e r a n

1. Angel
2. Ball
3. Bells
4. Box
5. Candle
6. Candy cane
7. Elf
8. Fireplace
9. Gingerbread man
10. Hat
11. Mittens
12. Reindeer
13. Santa
14. Snowflake
15. Star
16. Tree

DAY 6-Connect the dots!

Draw a line from dot number 1 to dot number 2, then from dot number 2 to dot number 3, 3 to 4, and so on. Continue to join the dots until you have connected all the numbered dots. Then color the picture!

DAY 7

Color the kitten!

DAY 8 — Write the total number of each item in the boxes. (Bonus: What is the total number of things?) Color the picture of Santa.

HOW MANY?

DAY 9 - Write the total number of winter things in each box. (Bonus: What is the total number of things?)

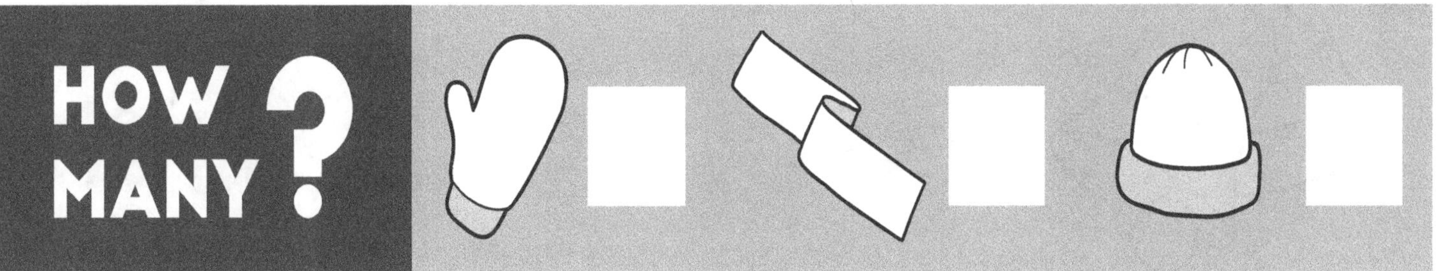

DAY 10 – Color, cut, and glue the bell on another sheet of paper.

DAY 11-Complete the Santa maze.

DAY 12-Color the gingerbread house.

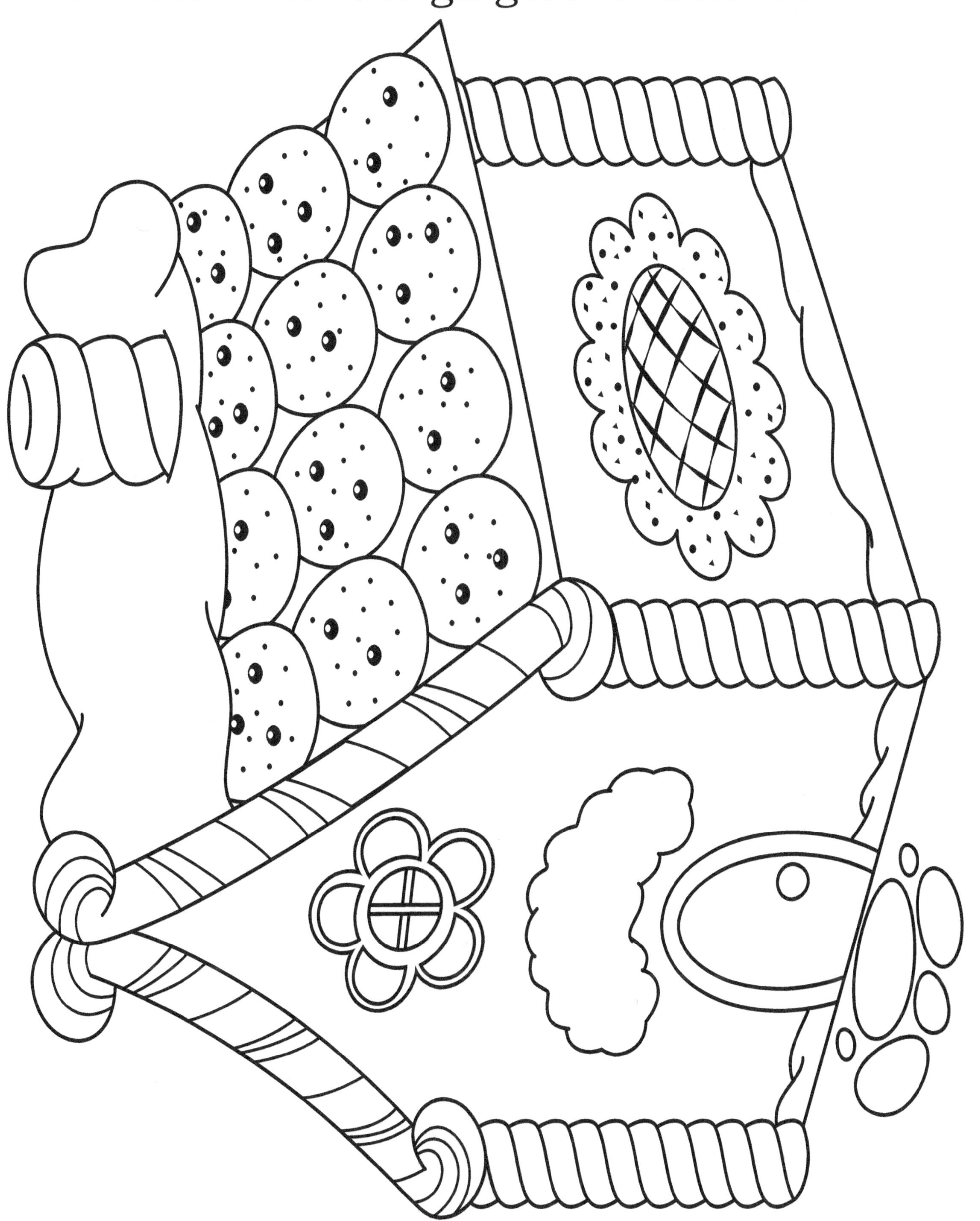

DAY 13

$$\bigcirc + \bigcirc + \bigcirc + \bigcirc = \bigcirc$$

0 1 2 3 4 5 6 7 8 9 + −

10 11 12 13 14 15 16 17 18 19 20 =

0 1 2 3 4 5 6 7 8 9

DAY 14-Connect the dots!

Draw a line from dot number 1 to dot number 2, then from dot number 2 to dot number 3, 3 to 4, and so on. Continue to join the dots until you have connected all the numbered dots. Then color the picture!

DAY 15 - Write the total of each group of ornaments in the boxes. (Bonus-What is the total number of ornaments?)

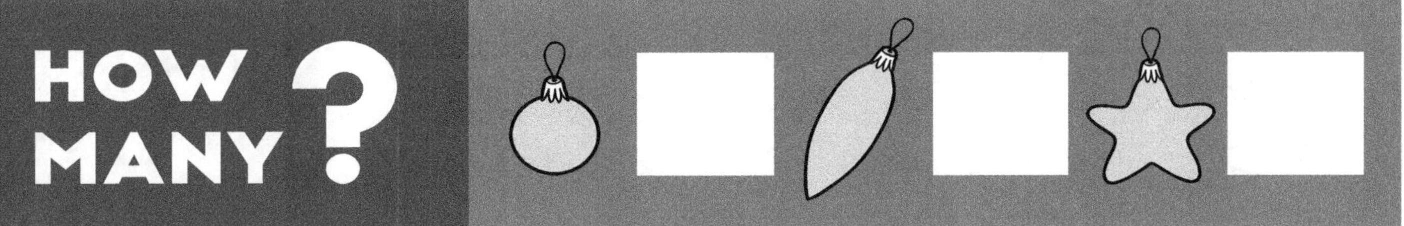

DAY 16-Color, cut, & glue Santa on another sheet of paper.

DAY 17-Complete the maze and color the tree!

DAY 18-Color the jolly Santa!

DAY 19-Color the three kings! Can you name the things in their hands?

DAY 20-Color, cut, & glue the gift on another sheet of paper.

DAY 21-Color the playful reindeer.

DAY 22-Compare the two pictures and color the silly Santas.

DAY 23-Connect the dots & color the tree.

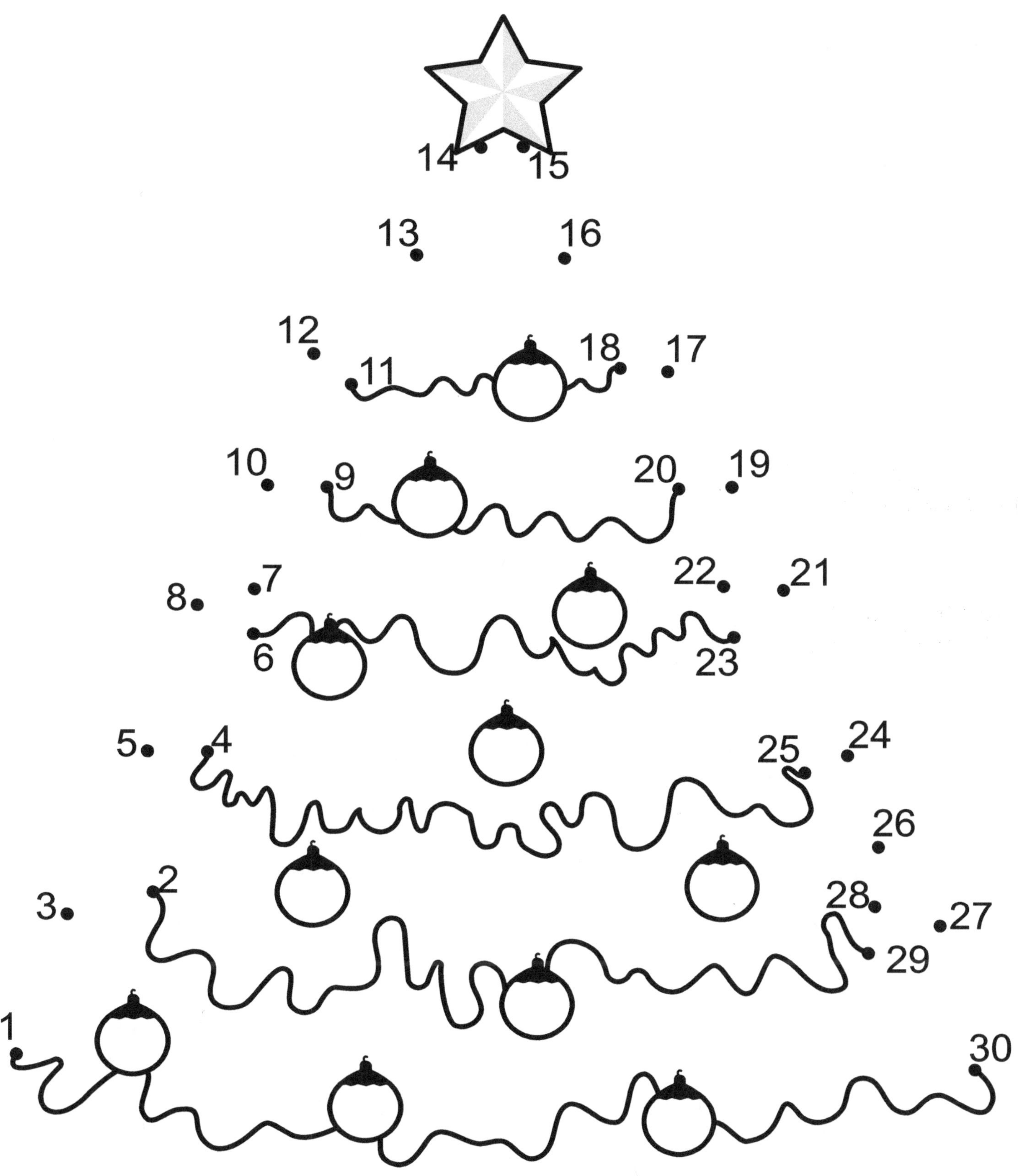

DAY 24-Use the grid as a guide to help you finish drawing the bell. Then color the bell.

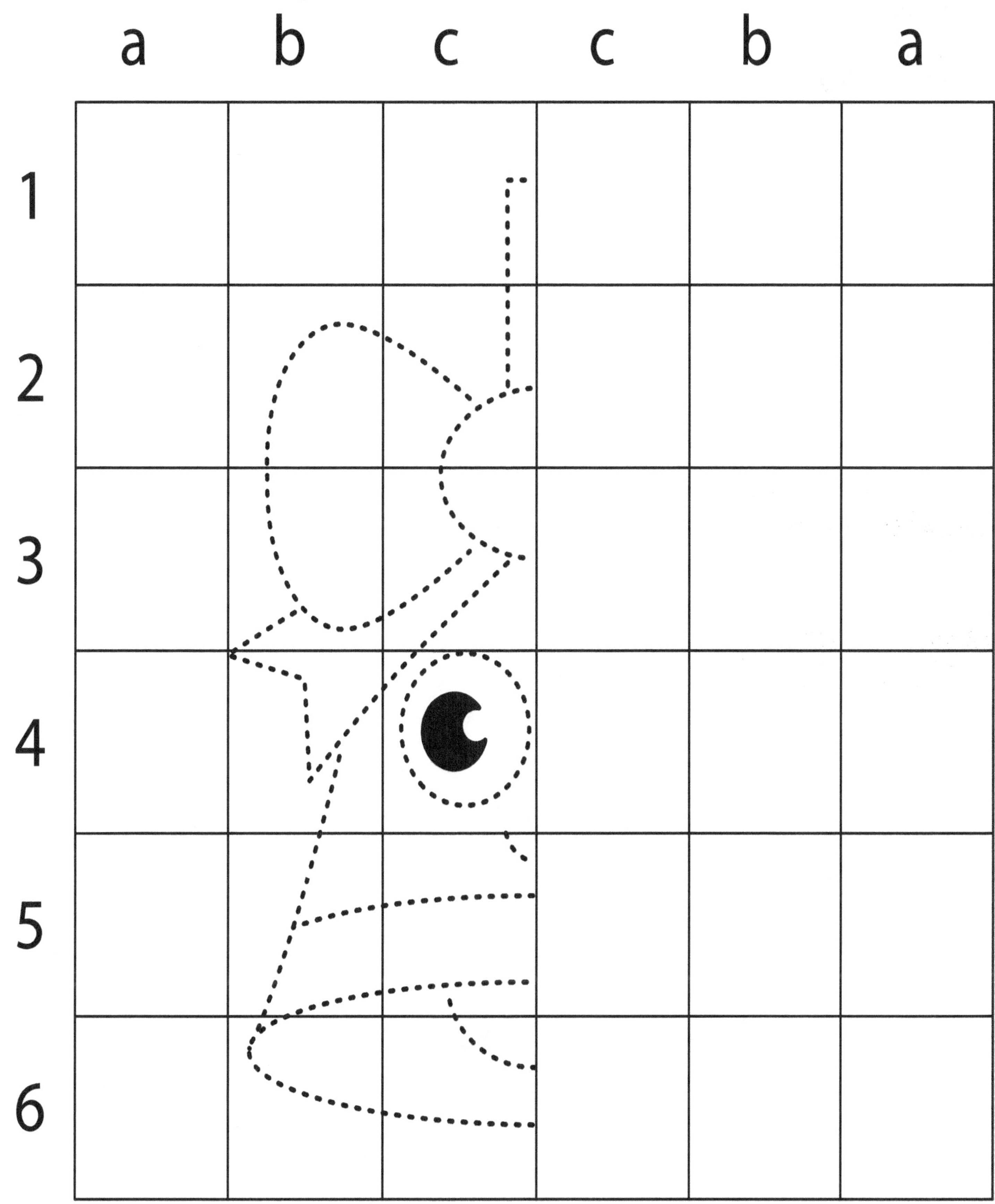

DAY 25-Color the fireplace, so it's decorated for Christmas. Did you remember to draw the stockings?

Color in each day during Advent. Then cut out the calendar and glue the days in the correct order on another sheet of paper.

Thank you for your purchase!
We hope you've been enjoying
your Advent Activity Book.

florabellapublishing.com
Florabella Publishing, LLC

www.ingramcontent.com/pod-product-compliance
Lightning Source LLC
Chambersburg PA
CBHW080814280726
48660CB00018B/3448